The Bible Book of Exodus Study Guide

Understanding God's Word

The Bible Book of Exodus Study Guide: Understanding God's Word

By Brian Gugas

First Print Edition

To my Parents,

Through all the Tough Phases of Life

Table of Contents

Introduction

When we think of the Bible we automatically think of the Church, God, Jesus, and words like religion, miracles, and faith. But the Bible is also perceived or viewed as a book of do's and don'ts. For some, these do's and don'ts are a much-appreciated guidebook or life GPS. For others, however, the wisdom and instruction found in the Bible is restrictive, old-fashioned, and senseless.

What we think about the Bible or how we view it, however, doesn't change its truth or its relevance. The absence of tangible proof that the miracles and many other events in the Bible too place does not mean this is proof of absence. Think about it like this: If you were sitting in your yard at night looking up at the sky just in time to see three shooting stars within a matter of a few seconds, would the fact that you had nothing but your word to prove that the event took place make it any less true? Of course not! The fact of the matter is that we do have a good deal of secular historical documentation that parallels to the truths and historical accounts contained in the Bible. But proving the truth of the Bible is not what this book is about.

This book, and the ones that follow for each of the other books in the Bible, is written for the purpose of providing a more in-depth understanding and knowledge of the Scriptures based upon the original text (language). This book is also for the purpose of teaching or reminding readers of the following facts about the Bible:

- The Bible is a unified text in that its theme is carried out from Genesis to Revelation without contradiction in spite of the fact that it was written over a period of several hundred years by a number of different writers.

- Each book, chapter, and verse hinges on the others; meaning none of the Bible can be isolated from the rest of it. The full meaning and 'story' is dependent on the whole text in order to be complete.

Scientists argue the exodus never happened—that it is all just a big myth of the Jewish culture. Their reasoning for this is that Egyptian history doesn't record any evidence of the plagues or the loss of so many members of its army in the Red Sea. Strangely enough, these same scientists admit that Egypt's ancient documentations of their history don't record ANY losses of battle or defeats of any kind that would have brought embarrassment to the Pharaoh or made him look weak; something the plagues and the Red Sea debacle would have done.

Scientists have also stated that no evidence of hundreds of thousands of people living in the Sinai Desert has been found. This is their 'proof' the Bible is untrue in regards to the account of the Israelites wandering for 40 years before finally entering the Promised Land. While it is true no great archeological findings have been made to prove there were settlements of large groups of people in the area, you need to keep the following in mind:

- The Israelites didn't settle in the desert—they traveled it for 40 long years. Because of their disobedience and lack of faith, the journey that should and could have taken only 11 days took 40 long, hot, eventful years.

- The Israelites did not embalm their dead or put them in a coffin. When you combine this fact with the fact that bodies decompose rapidly when exposed to heat, acidic ground, and other natural elements (all of which the Sinai Desert has to offer), it makes sense that the bodies of the Israelites who died within that 40 years have not been unearthed.

- Bodies buried directly in the ground as the Israelites were would undergo complete decomposition (including bones and teeth) within 200 to 300 years—long before anyone would be digging for evidence.

Other evidence to support the proof of the Bible's truth as written in the book of Exodus includes:

- Studies on the water level of the Nile River and ancient Egyptian history back up or coincide with the famine Joseph predicted and prepared for as recorded in Genesis, which is what led to the Israelite's coming to Egypt.
- Archeologists have uncovered bricks used in making the

> temples and pyramids of ancient Egypt with and without straw as recorded in Exodus.

As you read, read with your heart as well as your mind for the purpose of gaining knowledge, wisdom, and truth. But at the end of the day it all comes down to faith—choosing to believe in spite of the fact that you cannot see what you believe (Hebrews 11:1).

NOTE: The following websites offer more information on the research done to validate the proof of the Bible's truth.

http://www.arkdiscovery.com/joseph.htm

http://www.christiananswers.net/q-abr/abr-a027.html

BRIAN GUGAS

The Who, What, and Why of the Book of Exodus

The book of Exodus was written by Moses. It is another book that is labeled as one of the books of history in the Bible. It begins with a brief explanation of what happened in Egypt after Joseph and his brothers (the twelve tribes of Israel) passed away. This is followed by a brief listing of the family tree of a man named Moses—the man that was hand-picked by God to lead the Israelites out of Egypt. He would lead them back to the land of Canaan—the land God promised Abraham several hundred years prior to Moses' conversation with God.

From there the book takes us through the actual exodus (which means departure) of the Israelites from Egypt, and some of their wanderings through the desert.

Exodus is a book of history, but it is also a book filled with insights into God's holiness, his power, his unwillingness to accept anything other than complete obedience, and his tremendous love and his patience in waiting for his chosen people, Israel, to humble themselves to him completely.

The book of Exodus gives us an amazing up-close and personal look at the personality of God; starting with his name, I AM, and numerous reminders of why doing things God's way is always best.

With the exception of the first couple of chapters, Exodus can be described as a first-person account. Moses lived and breathed nearly everything written. And what he didn't remember could easily have been relayed to him via his parents and siblings.

BRIAN GUGAS

Population Explosion and Oppression

Exodus begins by reminding us of the names of Jacob's sons—the twelve tribes of Israel, and that once they and their families settled in Egypt, there were 70 of them in all (including Joseph, his wife, and 2 sons). I want to take you

now to where the story really begins—
verses 6-14...

 Now Joseph and all his brothers and all
that generation died, but the Israelites
were exceedingly fruitful; they
multiplied greatly, increased in
numbers and became so numerous that
the land was filled with them. Then a
new king, to whom Joseph meant
nothing, came to power in Egypt.
"Look," he said to his people, "the
Israelites have become far too numerous
for us. Come, we must deal shrewdly
with them or they will become even
more numerous and, if war breaks out,
will join our enemies, fight against us
and leave the country." So they put
slave masters over them to oppress
them with forced labor, and they built
Pithom and Rameses as store cities for
Pharaoh. But the more they were
oppressed, the more they multiplied

and spread; so the Egyptians came to dread the Israelites and worked them ruthlessly. They made their lives bitter with harsh labor in brick and mortar and with all kinds of work in the fields; in all their harsh labor the Egyptians worked them ruthlessly. (Exodus 1:6-14)

Okay, let's take this passage of scripture apart and examine it more closely…

The Israelites had a population explosion. While they still may have been considered a minority (technically speaking), the ratio of Israelites to Egyptians was becoming more balanced.

A new king (Pharaoh) came to power that didn't know anything about Joseph or what he had done. This is both feasible and disturbing.

The feasibility comes in the fact that we know Joseph lived another thirteen years after Jacob died while living in Egypt. In that thirteen years Joseph might easily have shifted his focus to his family since the drought had passed— reducing his presence and his power in the hierarchy of the government. This would explain why he didn't know Joseph. Another explanation of this could easily be attributed to the fact that the Egyptians were a people who prided themselves on being stronger, smarter, and more advanced than any other people group. So...if Joseph was identifying himself more with the Israelites at this point, the new Pharaoh would not have 'lowered' himself to give credit to anyone else for saving Egypt. And finally, we must remember that the rise to power was an inherited thing. It wasn't like the new Pharaoh had been running in political circles for years in order to attain the position he now held.

The disturbing factors of this statement are aimed at you and me. Studies show (The Pew Report and The Barna Group) that less than half of all teenagers who claim to be practicing Christians believe every word of the Bible to be true. This is beyond unacceptable to God and should be to us...to the church. For us to shake our heads wondering and questioning the reason why Joseph's contributions weren't remembered is nothing more than we are doing with God's Word.

The Egyptians were afraid of the Israelites because their population explosion was booming. They were afraid of being outnumbered if they decided to overthrow the government or join forces with another people group who wanted to do so. This tells us that the Israelites were savvy, strong, and productive. Otherwise they wouldn't have posed a threat. We sometimes mistakenly think the number of Israelites was HUGE. But that wasn't really the case—not to the extent we often think of, anyway. We will learn later on that on the night of the Exodus there were about 600,000 men plus the women, children, and non-Israelite people that went with them. But that 600,000 plus figure is mathematically possible based upon a birth rate of four children per family (many families had more) and the fact that people didn't live beyond 120 years. To show you what I mean, look at the chart put together by Wayne Blank:

How can a small group become a nation of millions in just over 4 centuries? A simple bit of arithmetic shows that it was easily possible. If the average Israelite family consisted of 4 children by the time the parents were 27 years old (the Bible record shows that families then were actually much larger), that would provide for a doubling of the population every 27 years (2 children to replace the parents, and 2 children to account for population growth). 430 years divided by 27 years is about 15 generations during the time Israel was in Egypt.

Beginning with the original 70 people, growth of the Israelite nation using our factors above would have been:

140 people after 27 years

280 people after 54 years

560 people after 81 years

1,120 people after 108 years

2,240 people after 135 years

4,480 people after 162 years

8,960 people after 189 years

17,920 people after 216 years

35,840 people after 243 years

71,680 people after 270 years

143,360 people after 297 years

286,720 people after 324 years

573,440 people after 351 years

1,146,880 people after 378 years

2,293,760 people after 405 years

Pharaoh nipped the problem in the bud by making slaves out of them. This begins the 400 year period of slavery we read about later on in Exodus. But God had plans for Israel—and a promise to keep. He had promised Abraham that he would be the father of a great and might nation and we all know that God doesn't break promises.

The plight of slavery didn't stop Israel from growing, so Pharaoh ordered the midwives to kill the boy babies when they delivered them. We don't know if the if the midwives were of Egyptian decent or not, but what we do know is this: the two midwives whose names are listed as Shiphrah and Puah disobeyed the Pharaoh by lying to him and letting the baby boys live.

In regards to the midwives t is interesting to note the following:

The names Shiphrah and Puah mean beauty and splendor. Their names denote the condition of their hearts toward the value of life and toward God.

The Bible tells us they feared the LORD. This lends itself to say they were Israelites or at least believers in God rather than the gods of the Egyptians.

We learn in verse 20 and 21 of chapter 1 that because they trusted God, God gave them families of their own. This would imply that midwives—at least these two—were infertile prior to this. God's blessing of giving them families of their own would have been significant in the fact that to be infertile was considered a shameful thing and grounds for your husband being able to divorce you; making you an outcast.

Many have wondered at how two midwives could possibly have cared for ALL the Israelite women having babies. The answer to that is this: in all likelihood, they weren't the only two midwives. They were most likely the head midwives and instructing the others to follow suit with their practices OR yes, they were the only midwives during that time period. Remember: the population explosion didn't happen overnight.

When all is said and done, God is going to have his way no matter what and no matter who tries to intervene. The Israelites were fertile and didn't experience the high infant mortality rate (naturally or imposed) because it wasn't part of God's plan. What was in his plan, however, was for a baby to be born that would pave the way for the Israelites to return to the land God wanted them to call their own.

BRIAN GUGAS

Moses...the Early Years

Chapter 2 begins with the account of Moses' birth and surviving the Pharaoh's orders that all baby boys be thrown into the Nile River to drown. The highlights of the story include:

Learning that Moses' parents were both from the tribe of Levi—the tribe designated as the priestly tribe. This is significant in the fact that Moses would be their physical and spiritual leader throughout the Exodus and that job could technically only go to a Levite. What's more, Moses' brother Aaron, along with his sons, were designated as the head priests among the Israelites on their journey across the desert—something else that could have only been done by a Levite.

Moses' mother and father (whose names we later learn are Amram and Jochebed) defy the order to let their infant son be drowned and hide him until he can no longer be easily hidden (about 3 months, according to 2:2).

Jochebed puts the baby in a basket and sets the basket afloat in the very river he would have been drowned in and leaves her young daughter to watch over him.

The Pharaoh's daughter finds the baby in the basket while bathing in the river and decides to adopt the baby as her own. It's obvious that the baby is not Egyptian, but that doesn't matter to this woman. This fact gives evidence of God's divine intervention by giving him insight into both societies and preserving his life for what lie ahead.

Miriam (the baby's sister) steps forward and volunteers to find someone to nurse the baby. Of course she takes her brother home to their mother, who raises him as an Israelite with an Egyptian future.

It is important to stop here and consider the following: Some people believe the Levite tribe was exempted from slavery—that even Pharaoh respected the religious rights of others. This would explain why Jochebed was allowed to raise the baby as her own rather than be raised by an Egyptian wet nurse. The fact that Jochebed was paid (vs. 9) to raise the baby also lends weight to the fact that she and her family were not slaves in the truest form of the word.

When the baby grew older, the Bible says, he was taken to Pharaoh's daughter and he became her son. And SHE named him Moses.

Did you get that—SHE, as in the Pharaoh's daughter—named him Moses because Moses means 'drawn out of the water'.

This opens the door to several questions. Some we have answers to and some we don't.

Question 1: What was Moses' name before he went to live with his adoptive mother?

Answer 1: We don't know. But here is what we do know:

*We are not given a name prior to the Bible telling us the Pharaoh's daughter named him Moses. This indicates that any prior name he had didn't matter.

*The name Moses is equivalent to the Hebrew name Mosheh, which means 'draw out'. This could indicate the he was 'renamed' Moses instead of Mosheh in order to make him 'more officially' Egyptian and hers.

*The name Moses or forms of it was commonly used in Egyptian royalty. This indicates the love she felt for the baby and the hope she had for his future.

*This was the name he (Moses) identified with.

Question 2: How long did Moses live with his biological family before going to live with the Pharaoh's family?

Answer 2: Somewhere between 2 and 3 years. This is based on other Biblical accounts of children being weaned, which is the most logical time for him to have left his biological mother.

Question 3: How did Moses' Egyptian mother get away with bringing a Hebrew boy into the family?

Answer 3: The Bible calls this woman Pharaoh's daughter—not one of his daughters, but his daughter. This implies she was his only daughter which would possibly mean she held a special place in his heart. Remember...Egyptian women were valued by their male counterparts in ways most other cultures didn't embrace. She was obviously a soft-hearted and compassionate young woman. What else besides her gentle nature and personality would have led her to go to such care to love a Hebrew baby so much that she would adopt him? When you put all of this together you get a kind, loving young woman whose father obviously respected her for who she was and was willing to make an exception to a rule he made for the daughter he loved.

We end the 'early years' of Moses with the event that causes him to leave Egypt—literally running for his life...

From a toddler being taken to his royal home we jump to Moses as an adult going out to watch the Hebrews working under the oppression of their Egyptian masters. The Bible tells us that on this particular day he witnessed an Egyptian beating a Hebrew slave. Moses knew he was adopted and that he was biologically one of these oppressed people, so seeing the slave being beaten did not set well with him. In fact, he was so enraged that he killed the Egyptian and hid his body in the sand.

He hid the body in the sand. This is such a simple statement, but one that actually says quite a bit. Hiding the body in the sand was exactly what needed to be done in order to ensure the evidence of the murder (the body) decomposed as quickly as possible. To put the body in the mud pits or even to dig a grave and bury him would have greatly increased the odds of the body being found before it was nothing but bones.

Now think back...what did we say about the lack of evidence of there being a 40 year journey made through the desert? Do you see it? God provides countless subtle statements such as this one throughout the Bible that serve to add validity to the evidences scientists seek to find to prove and disprove the Bible. But the 'funny' thing is...every single one of these statements adds weight to the side of truth...lots of weight.

We don't know what happened to the Israelite who was being beat. Maybe Moses waited until he/she had left the scene. Since we are told Moses looked this way and that to make sure there were no witnesses, this is the most plausible explanation.

The next verse tells us that Moses didn't look this way and that hard enough, because the very next day when Moses was once again walking in and among the Hebrews, it became evident that there were witnesses to the crime he had committed. Two Hebrews, who were fighting among themselves called Moses on the carpet, so to speak, when he broke up a fight between them.

One of the men involved in the fight asked if Moses was going to kill him like he'd killed the Egyptian. This statement is followed by one that tells us the Pharaoh found out about it too—proof that news travels fast...even between slaves and their masters. At this point we see the Pharaoh express feelings of bias and prejudice against his adopted Hewbrew grandchild in the fact that he wanted to kill him. This is when Moses literally runs for his life and runs as far and as fast as he can from Egypt.

A New Life and a Calling Like None Other

Moses left Egypt and went to Midian. Midian is on the other side of the Red Sea from Egypt, although it is reachable without crossing the body of water — which is most likely the case with

Moses. Midian is south of Edom and southeast of Goshen, which is where (or near) Moses was when he fled his homeland.

The trip wasn't a quick one by any stretch of the imagination. Moses was crossing the dessert—the same one he would cross back over 40 years later and then cross over again on his way to the Promised Land with those entrusted to his care by God. The geographical distance between the two locations would require approximately 150 days of walking at a rate of 8 hours a day.

Some might wonder why Midian? Was that his intended destination or did he just end up there?

There is no way to know for sure, but it was most likely the first place he came to that offered prospects of living a productive, self-sufficient life. Moses was undoubtedly highly educated in a variety of subjects, but let's face it—as royalty he didn't have much (if any) experience in manual labor or providing for himself. Midian might have been the first place he came to that he thought held the promise of something more than that.

Another possibility is that Moses didn't necessarily intend to stay in Midian—that it just worked out the way because of the following incident.

Moses came to a well where some young women were watering their sheep. While they were busy getting the job done, another group of shepherds—men—came to water their sheep. Not wanting to wait, they pushed the young women aside; telling them they would have to wait. Moses, being the champion of the underdog he obviously was, came to the girls' rescue and watered their sheep for them.

A champion of underdogs...that was Moses. He committed murder because he was standing up for the underdog (an Israelite slave). He ran away from home after breaking up a fight between two slaves in order to avoid being killed by the Pharaoh. He returned to Egypt to be the hands, feet, and mouth of God to rescue the underdogs (Israelites).

The young women he helped turned out to be the daughters of the Midianite priest, Jethro. At their invitation, Moses went home with the girls to meet their father and have dinner. That dinner invitation ended up giving Moses a lot more than dinner. Moses married one of Jethro's daughters—Zipporah. Moses also took the job of shepherd for his father in-law and he and Zipporah had two sons. F

Moses spent a total of 40 years in Midian with Zipporah and her family and it was at the end of that40 years that Moses received the call of a lifetime.

Moses was a spry 80 year-old when God spoke to him from a burning bush one day while Moses was out tending to Jethro's sheep. Exodus 3:1 is one of those verses where God puts in another subtle statement of proof that he is the true author of the Bible. It is a simple statement that is easily overlooked if you are just reading to get to the exciting part of the story. But if you are really taking in each word, you would have to stop and ask yourself why he has Moses refer to Mt. Horeb (where Moses and the sheep are when God appears to him) as the "…mountain of God."

When Moses wrote the book of Exodus he would understand why God would see fit to refer to Mt. Horeb as the Mountain of God, but not even Moses knew just how special the mountain would be even after the experiences he had there. Only God knew what was coming to make the name even more appropriate (if that is possible).

What was so special about it? The answer is that Mt. Horeb is the site of the majority of major events in the Old Testament and a few in the New Testament as well. Mt. Horeb, which is also known as Mt. Sinai, is where God gave Moses the Ten Commandments, the Law, and instructions for building the Tabernacle. It is the site of Moses and Jethro's meeting on how to govern the people. It is where Elijah called down fire from heaven to prove God is real and Baal is not. It is the site of the transfiguration Jesus allowed Peter, James, and John to witness.

It is also very important to note that Mt. Horeb was not in Jethro's backyard. It wasn't as if Moses was taking the sheep out each morning to graze and bringing them back to the barn lot at night. That's not how it worked (or how it works even still today, for that matter). The terrain of the area would necessitate having rotational grazing schedule — grazing a large area of ground then moving on to the next and then the next and so forth until you eventually made your way back to where you started. This would allow the ground to recover and fresh grass for grazing to be available when you got there. I tell you this to emphasize the point that while Mt. Horeb is in Midian, it was most likely not situated as such that Moses was home with the family that night — giving him time to digest everything that happens to him there before he gets home and has to try to explain it all to his family.

Anyway...Moses was tending sheep somewhere on Mt. Horeb when God called to him from a burning bush that wasn't turning to charred wood in spite of it being on fire. When Moses walked over to investigate, God called Moses by name and Moses answered. The next few minutes (which probably seemed like hours to Moses) can be summed up as follows:

Moses answers and is told to take off his shoes because he is standing on holy ground.

God reveals his identity; saying he is the God of Abraham, Isaac, and Jacob.

Moses hides his face in reverence and fear—evidence that he knew of God

God tells Moses why he is there—to tell Moses to go back to Egypt to rescue the Israelites from slavery in Egypt.

Moses doesn't hesitate to tell God he's got the wrong guy for the job.

God tells Moses not to worry—that he will be with him every step of the way.

Moses tries a second time to get out of it—in a sort of sneaky way. He asks God who he (Moses) is supposed to say sent him when the Israelites ask.

God answers I AM.

Moses tries twice more to get God to send someone else before finally saying (4:13) "Oh, LORD, please send someone else to do it."

Throughout the conversation between Moses and God, God performs a couple of miracles to prove to Moses that a) he is capable of doing what he says he is going to do b) to prove to Moses he is really God

God, who has been the epitome of patience and reassurance becomes angry at Moses but concedes to let his brother Aaron be the spokesman for them. He makes it very clear, however, that Aaron is the 'mouth of Moses' but that Moses is the one through which God will work—and that he will use Moses' staff to do much of that work.

Let's stop a minute before we move forward to what happens after the burning bush—mainly to talk about Aaron and Aaron and Moses' relationship...

When God agrees to take some of the burden off of Moses by allowing Aaron to be the spokesman, God tells Moses that Aaron is already on his way to meet up with Moses (4:14) and that he is excited to see him. The fact that Aaron was already on his way (which is recorded later on in chapter 4) provides further evidence that one of three things was going on:

The Levites were not subjected to the slave labor the other tribes were.

Special treatment being shown to Moses' 'foster' family—which is not likely the case given the fact that the Pharaoh in power when Moses left wanted him dead.

God's divine and supernatural intercession allowed Aaron to travel to Midian to meet Moses.

Another question this brings up is whether or not Moses had been in contact with Aaron over the years. You need to remember that at this point Moses had been gone from Egypt 40 years. How much time and what options did he have for communicating with his biological family during this period of time?

The answer is that we simply don't know. We just know that they met as brothers and that is really all we need to know.

Moses does return to Jethro, Zipporah, and his sons, tells them what happened and basically asks Jethro's permission to leave. Jethro, who has proven and will continue to prove himself to be a wise and Godly man, gives Moses his blessing to return to his people. And so they leave.

Exodus 4:24-26 gives us a brief glimpse into the first leg of the journey—one that seems very random and strange, but as is always the case with God, has definite purpose and meaning. Let's look at those verses:

At a lodging place on the way, the Lord met Moses and was about to kill him. But Zipporah took a flint knife, cut off her son's foreskin and touched Moses' feet with it. "Surely you are a bridegroom of blood to me," she said. So the Lord let him alone. (At that time she said "bridegroom of blood," referring to circumcision.)

Why would God kill Moses after insisting he go to Egypt?

Much study has been devoted to these verses. What follows is a summation of a compilation of the thoughts and conclusions by a number of theologians.

The Hebrew text for the phrase 'about to kill him' is more accurately translated 'would have killed him'. But again, why? In short, God was not willing to allow Moses to lead Israel if he couldn't even lead his own family in being fully obedient to God.

That's right—the fact that one of Moses' sons was not circumcised was a blatant act of disobedience to God. God had established this sign of obedience with Abraham and stated that it was to be carried out always and forever. And God needed Moses to be in full compliance. How else could he be deserving of the respect of the Israelites?

That being said...Moses was traveling with his Midianite wife, Zipporah and his two sons. The fact that Zipporah was a Midianite meant that the act of circumcision was not something she would have found necessary. Since she only circumcised one of the boys, it is reasonable to assume that Moses had insisted the oldest boy, Gerhsom, had been circumcised as a baby like all Hebrew (Israelite) baby boys were, but that Zipporah had not consented to having her youngest (Eliezar) subjected to the painful and seemingly senseless procedure. So when the Bible tells us that God would have or was about to kill Moses, we need to know and believe that God was giving Moses and Zipporah a chance to come to the place of full obedience. Had he not complied, God might very well have killed Moses and chosen someone else for the job. He would simply have chosen someone who was willing to obey God down to the smallest detail.

Zipporah was obviously privy to what was going on stepped up to do what needed to be done. This actually says quite a bit about Zipporah's character. While she may not have approved of or understood the act of circumcision, she obviously loved her husband enough to leave the only home she had ever known and do what needed to be done to save him from God's wrath.

Zipporah's act (circumcising their son) brought Moses into full compliance, God was pleased and Moses went on his way.

An Israelite Reunion and Meeting Pharaoh

As promised by God, Aaron met Moses near the Mountain of God, the two brothers had a heart-felt reunion, Moses told Aaron everything God had said and done when he was there earlier and then the two made their way back to Egypt.

FYI: You will notice that no mention is made of Zipporah and the boys being with Moses. This is mentioned later on in Exodus, but the most plausible reason they weren't with him is that after the circumcision of their son, the journey would have been too much for him. They most likely stayed behind for him to heal and then returned to Jethro's household to wait for Moses to send for them.

Once Moses and Aaron arrive back in Egypt, chapter 5 finds them telling the Israelites that God had heard their cries for help and was going to take them from this awful place. Upon hearing this, the Bible tells us they believed and worshipped God.

Immediately after that, we see Moses and Aaron going before Pharaoh. The first request they make is for Pharaoh to let the people go so they can go worship God in the desert. Pharaoh refuses. They ask again—for permission to take the people on a 3-day journey into the dessert. This time they tell him that they need to offer sacrifices to God or else they may suffer God's wrath through plagues or the sword. Pharaoh refuses again and complains that Moses and Aaron would be taking the people away from the work he needs them to do.

Directly following this first meeting, Pharaoh orders his slave drivers to make things even harder on the Israelites. He instructs them to make the people work harder by having to gather their own straw to make the bricks WITHOUT reducing their quota. But the slave drivers go one 'better'. They make the Israelites make their bricks without any straw at all and to do it without reducing their daily quota. If they didn't do it, the Israelite foremen appointed by Pharaoh were beaten.

When the Israelite foremen realized why they were being penalized (because of Moses and Aaron's request to take the people into the desert), they let Moses and Aaron know they did not appreciate being the brunt of Pharaoh's anger and to leave them alone. Moses, who is understandably upset and a bit confused, asks God why this is happening.

Before we go any deeper into the events that lead to the actual exodus, let's take a minute to address the question some people have about why Moses and Aaron asked only to take the people out to worship rather than not demanding their release right up-front.

If you will notice in this first meeting with Pharaoh, Moses never infers that they will return. He simply tells Pharaoh the people need to be allowed to leave so that they can worship God fully, purposefully, and without the interference of work. Pharaoh is told they want to travel a distance that is a 3 day journey from where they are, but again, he never says they will be coming back.

As to why they don't just come right out and tell Pharaoh they don't plan on coming back, one can assume any or all of the following reasons apply to why God didn't have them do so:

It isn't wise to reveal your 'game plan' to the opposing team.

God was testing Pharaoh; giving him a chance to do things peacefully.

God was baiting Pharaoh so that either his army would accompany them or go after them; allowing God to deal with 'only' the army rather than making all of Egypt suffer for Pharaoh's prideful disobedience.

Whatever the reason, Pharaoh's heart and mind was not pliable or open to God's leading so when Moses asked God he was allowing things to get even worse for the Israelites, God basically told Moses, "You ain't seen nothin' yet." He tells Moses that to Abraham, Isaac, Jacob, and the Israelites (to this point) he has been known as God Almighty, but that they will now know him as LORD (Yahweh) (Jehovah).

The exact translation of the phrase 'known to them' in the Hebrew language means to have an intellectual knowledge of something, or in this case, someone. In other words, prior to what was about to take place they knew God was God and that he was LORD, but they did not yet have a clear picture of what being LORD really meant—what power and holiness he possessed.

This is important in order to erase any doubt about the Bible contradicting itself since Genesis is filled with references to God as LORD. When God is called LORD in Genesis, you need to keep in mind that it is Moses writing and he was writing after God had made himself known as LORD to the Israelites. But he is also called LORD by Abraham—the first reference being in Genesis 14:22 and then shortly thereafter in 15:2. So when you take in the big picture, I'll say it again… prior to what was about to take place they knew God was God and that he was LORD, but they did not yet have a clear picture of what being LORD really meant—what power and holiness he possessed.

During this conversation, God also instructed Moses to tell the Israelites they that he was taking them to the Promised Land he had promised Abraham. Moses obeyed, but the people refused to believe him. They were so discouraged and suffering somewhat from what we now call Stockholm syndrome—being attached or dependent on the person or people holding you hostage or enslaving you.

When Moses told God the people wouldn't believe him (as if he didn't already know), God told him to go back to Pharaoh and tell Pharaoh to let the Israelites leave…for good.

The Plagues

Now we come to the most popular or well-known part of the book of Exodus...the plagues. God used a series of ten plagues to humble Egypt into letting the Israelites leave the country and be free from slavery. The plagues were varied in nature and assaulted the people from every direction.

Setting the stage

Right before God begins his barrage of trouble, he speaks to Moses; telling him three very important things we are going to look at before we talk about the plagues themselves.

#1: God tells Moses he is making him (Moses) like God in Pharaoh's eyes (7:1). In the next sentence, God says that Aaron will be Moses' prophet, so to speak, since he will be the one doing most of the talking. These statements are significant in the fact that they elevate Moses and Aaron to a higher status than any human has ever been to this point. We are all called to be like God in the way we love others and conduct our lives, but this is different. God is, for the first time, using someone (Moses) as an instrument for his miracles. To this point God has done them himself. This time he is going to reveal himself through Moses and Aaron is going to be the one telling Pharaoh what God expects the people of Egypt to learn from their experiences.

This event has both literal and figurative significance in that it accomplishes what God sets out to do (literal) and is a foreshadowing of what is to come in a little over a thousand years (figurative).

#2: God hardens Pharaoh's heart. I'll be honest. Exodus 7:3 is one of the most questioned and controversial verses in the Bible—it and the others referencing the fact that God hardened Pharaoh's heart over the course of time when the plagues took place. And I admit, it has stymied and even frightened me. After all, if God would harden one person's heart, what would keep him from hardening someone else's...possibly even mine?

In my studies to find an answer to this question I have found those that believe God couldn't have deliberately hardened Pharaoh's heart. If he did, it would nullify the free-will God already had in place. Others believe he purposefully did harden Pharaoh's heart for the purpose of revealing his power and holiness to a very superstitious and idol-worshipping people. So which is right?

The Bible clearly states in no uncertain terms that God hardens the heart of Pharaoh. He hardened it SO THAT Pharaoh and the people of Egypt would know without a doubt that God is who he says he is and that he is the one true God. There are also instances when the Bible says that Pharaoh hardens his own heart and those that simply say his heart was hardened. Each time this is mentioned the original Hebrew text uses a form of the word that means obstinate or stubborn.

What the Bible doesn't say, however, is how God hardened Pharaoh's heart. We just automatically assume God put some kind of 'lock' on Pharaoh's heart so that he wouldn't let the people of Israel go until God had done the absolute worst thing there was to do to the Egyptians — kill their children. But did he really do that? God is capable of that and might have done so. I say this because as the account of the plagues unfolds we see that:

The severity of the plagues increases

The plagues take different directions in regards to how they affect the Egyptians

The last plague is unmistakably symbolic of what will be the ultimate 'exodus from sin' (salvation through the blood of the perfect lamb, Jesus)

But I think we need to look at a possible alternative, as well. Rather than putting a lock on Pharaoh's heart, I believe it is quite possible that God simply didn't impose himself or force himself into the heart of a man who was already stubbornly turned against him—just like he doesn't force himself on us. He let Pharaoh be his own worst enemy.

I realize that brings up the question of why it specifically states that God hardened his heart in some places and in others, that Pharaoh did it to himself. I would answer that by saying the times Pharaoh hardened his own heart were after Moses stopped some of the plagues. It was a case of believing in God when you are in real need, but as soon as things get better, you forget he is there and go back to your old ways. In other words, Pharaoh did harden his own heart by choosing to ignore what he had witnessed in regards to the mighty holiness of God. God's actions (the plagues) hardened Pharaoh's heart by making him angrier and more resentful of God's power vs. the 'power' of the Egyptian gods and of Pharaoh himself.

Either way, Pharaoh acknowledged God as God when he had to in order to get relief but chose not to obey God. And yes, there is a HUGE difference between acknowledging and obeying.

#3: Pharaoh's magicians are able to duplicate some of the plagues. This is both interesting and somewhat comical in an ironic sort of way.

We read in chapters 7 and 8 that when Moses and Aaron went to Pharaoh and he asked for a miracle, Aaron threw down his staff and became a snake. Pharaoh's magicians, using their 'secret arts' (7:11) did the same thing. But...Aaron's snake swallowed theirs up.

Next, when Moses and Aaron inflicted the first two plagues upon Egypt, Pharaoh's magicians duplicated the plagues. This means they (the magicians) added to the bloodiness of the water and increased the number of frogs in Egypt. Talk about kicking a 'guy' when he's down! The magicians were making things worse for their own people and themselves!

Never mind why they did it. The question most people have is how they did it. The answer has to be one of two things: 1) God gave them the power to do so as part of his 'big picture plan' to humble Pharaoh. 2) Don't underestimate the power of Satan.

We know God has the power to do what he wants, when he wants, with or through whoever he wants. So if God wanted to use Pharaoh's magicians to make a statement or two…he could. But because God did not take credit for their handiwork, the next explanation is the one many scholars tend to believe to be the right one.

Satan has a lot of power here on earth. The Bible tells us in the books of 1st John, Jude, and Revelation that Satan does have power and influence in the global world. The fact that the Egyptians were a very superstitious, mystic sort of people who put a tremendous amount of confidence in the spirit world and magic, it would be completely reasonable to assume they were putty in Satan's hands and that he worked through them.

The so-called bottom line of their magic, though, is this: It only made matters worse and it had its limits.

The ten plagues

The ten plagues God sent upon Egypt were as follows:

Water to blood

Frogs

Gnats (lice)

Flies

Diseased livestock

Boils

Hail and fire

Locusts

Darkness

Death of the firstborn

Now let's list them again along with the key events surrounding each one.

Water to blood: 1st plague, duplicated by the magicians.

Frogs: Magicians also duplicated this plague. Pharaoh told Moses and Aaron to pray to the LORD to take them away and that if they did, he would allow them to take the people out of Goshen to make their sacrifices to God. Moses agreed and even told Pharaoh he could select the time for them to do so. Once the plague had ended and the frogs were nothing more than piles of stinky dead amphibians, "…he hardened his heart" (8:15) and wouldn't let them go.

Gnats: This is the first plague the magicians could not duplicate. When Aaron struck the ground, the dust flew up and became gnats—covering everyone and everything in Egypt. The magicians acknowledged the plague to be the work of God, but Pharaoh's stubbornness caused him to not budge.

Flies: This is the first plague that affected ONLY the Egyptians. God told Moses that he would not allow the flies to affect the land of Goshen where the Israelites lived. This, God said, would be a miraculous sign Pharaoh wouldn't be able to deny. When the swarms of flies appeared, Pharaoh tried to bargain with Moses; telling him they could make sacrifices to God in Egypt. Moses told Pharaoh those terms were not acceptable—that they needed to take that 3 day journey. Pharaoh counter-offered by saying they could leave Egypt to make their sacrifices, but they couldn't go far. Moses agreed, but warned Pharaoh not to go back on his word, which is exactly what he did.

Livestock: This is also the first plague that is not stopped when Moses asks God to do so. It was most likely a sickness that struck them all at once and then ended. God sent a plague on the livestock (camels, cattle, horses, donkeys, sheep, and goats) of the Egyptians. The next day, at the prescribed time, God sent the plague and most of the livestock belonging to the Egyptians died, but not one animal belonging to an Israelite died (9:5-7). Some translations and versions say "ALL the livestock died", which then causes confusion when you read about the next plague. But it needn't do so because the Hebrew word used here is KOL, which means 'all over' 'all sorts of', or 'from all over'. So when we read "all the livestock", the word 'all' is not literally ALL.

Boils: This is the first plague that directly affected the people physically. God had Aaron grab handfuls of soot from the furnace and throw it in the air in the presence of Pharaoh. When he did, boils instantly covered the skin of the people and animals that had not died as a result of the previous plague. This was one more time God hardened Pharaoh's heart, though, so he refused to listen to Moses and Aaron.

Hail: This is the first plague with a personal message from God to Pharaoh. It is a message that actually answers a few questions we've already talked about...and a few others we will have later on. Here is what God says to Pharaoh (by way of Moses): "But I have raised you up for this very purpose, that I might show you my power and that my name might be proclaimed in the all the earth...." (9:16) Did you catch that?

God said that he had put Pharaoh in the position he was in because he knew he would be able to use Pharaoh's stubborn pride to prove that he is the Almighty God. Now…think back to the discussion we had a few pages ago about why/if/how God hardened Pharaoh's heart. It answers the question of if and why God did it: yes, he did and because it was all part of the plan. The plague of hail killed anyone and anything not protected by shelter—even stripping the leaves and bark from the trees(9:19). Now this is where it gets a little more interesting. In verse 20 we read that Pharaoh's officials "…who feared the word of the LORD…" brought their slaves and livestock under shelter. What does this say to you? It should tell you that some of Pharaoh's officials had been convinced of the reality and power of God and that they were tired of suffering because of

Pharaoh's arrogant pride. What follows in the remainder of the chapter is even more interesting and can best be summed up as follows: Pharaoh calls Moses and Aaron to 'ask' them to go to God on his behalf to stop the hail. But this time, Pharaoh admitted he was in the wrong! Pharaoh actually admits he has sinned and tells Moses he can take the Israelites and leave. Once again, however, his remorse doesn't last. As soon as the hail stops, he changes his mind.

NOTE: An interesting, "oh, by the way" type of thing is inserted into verse 31 informs us that while the flax and barley was destroyed, the wheat and spelt were not because these crops weren't ripe yet. The fact that this was so randomly placed AND put in parentheses is somewhat of an oddity at first glance. I personally believe it was

God's way of showing Pharaoh (and us) just how exact and intentional he is and his way of letting us know he wasn't done with Egypt yet.

Locusts: Before God sends the locusts to destroy what little is left to destroy in the way of plants and trees, God reveals yet another reason for hardening Pharaoh's heart. The reason: so that not only will Pharaoh and those living in Egypt at that time will know that God is God, but they will tell their children and grandchildren about the things God did to humble them and prove his identity. This is also the first plague in which Pharaoh's officials stand up to Pharaoh; telling him enough is enough. They tell him to let the Israelites go before Egypt is ruined beyond repair. Knowing his officials are right, Pharaoh calls Moses and Aaron back to him and begins bargaining with them again. In the end no 'deal' was made and locusts cover everything. They devour every piece of fruit and everything green in Egypt. It is an event that will never be duplicated again (10:14-15). Pharaoh once again admits he is guilty of sinning against their God and asks that Moses and Aaron pray on his behalf. They do, God sends a great wind to remove the locusts, and Pharaoh is still adamant in his refusal to let the Israelites leave.

Darkness: This is the first plague God used to 'attack' the core beliefs of Egyptian idol worship. The Egyptians' primary god was Ra, the sun god. He was to the Egyptians what Zeus was to the Greeks. The Egyptians were truly worshippers of the sun and light, so when the Bible describes the darkness God sent over Egypt as a darkness that could be felt he means that in both a literal and figurative sense. It was literally so dark for three days that the Egyptians could not see their hand in front of their face. It was that in-a-cave-with-no-light kind of darkness. The fact that the darkness came on instantaneously was felt mentally and spiritually as a supernatural detachment. They had fallen from the good graces of Ra. The Israelites did not experience the darkness, though, which only served to make the situation even more disturbing to the highly superstitious people. This plague was (almost) the last straw for Pharaoh. Ra was everything to a Pharaoh, so to be covered in darkness was a serious matter. It was at this point that Pharaoh made a 'final offer' to Moses and Aaron. He told them they could take all the Israelites and leave, BUT that they had to leave their flocks and herds there. Moses would not agree to this, saying they needed some of the animals for their sacrifices. At this point Pharaoh told Moses and Aaron to leave and never come back. He told them that if he saw them again they would be killed.

The death of the firstborn: The final plague. This was the one that would secure the release of the Israelites from Egypt. It was also the plague that initiated the most sacred of Jewish customs and holidays (still practiced today) AND the plague that foreshadowed what was to come when the Messiah, Jesus...the first and only born son of God was offered up as the sacrificial lamb for the sins of the world. Prior to the final plague, God tells Moses that this is going to be it—that after this one final plague, Pharaoh and all of Egypt will know that he is God. God also has an extensive 'to do' list for Moses and the Israelites, as this is the night their lives will change forever.

The book of Exodus is true and accurate. But for those who doubt or who are working toward the goal of sharing this truth with others, archeological evidence supports the account of the plagues. One of those sources is "The Riddle of the Exodus" by James D. Long. Scientists have also found evidence of the plagues but prefer to try to explain it away scientifically rather than give credit where credit is due. Their ability to do so falls short, however. But that should come as no surprise to anyone, now should it?

BRIAN GUGAS

The Passover and the Night of Exodus

The Passover was different from the other plagues in the fact that it didn't happen quickly. There was a period of preparation for the Israelites prior to that horrible night of death. The total number of days it took to prepare for the death angel was fourteen days. During that time it is easy to believe that

Pharaoh might have started feeling at least a little bit victorious. Oh, it was true his land and his people had suffered greatly, but they were still standing and knowing what we know about him, it is equally easy to believe that he was planning his revenge on Moses, Aaron, and the Israelites who he felt were to blame for the calamity they had suffered.

Instructions for the Israelites

God gave the following instructions to Moses to give to the Israelites about the night of the Passover. Most of these instructions are still followed today by the Jewish religion.

The day God spoke to Moses regarding the Passover became the first day of the first month of the Jewish year. It is the month of Nisan.

On the 10th day of the month each Israelite family was to select a year-old male lamb or goat without defect. They were to take care of the lamb/goat for 4 days.

On the 14th day all Israelite families were to slaughter their lamb or goat at twilight. The Hebrew word for twilight means between the evenings, so we don't have a precise time, but traditionally it is late afternoon/early evening.

EVERY Israelite household was to 'paint' the top and sides of their doorframes with the blood of their slaughtered animal. This was a sign to the death angel not to kill the firstborn of the family living in that house.

The Israelites were to roast the lamb/goat. God was specific in saying they weren't to eat it raw or boil it...head, legs, and inner parts (12:9). They were to eat it with unleavened bread and bitter herbs. The unleavened bread symbolized the need for expediency in leaving. They didn't have time to let their bread rise before baking it. The bitter herbs were probably green onions and horseradish. They symbolize the bitterness of being held as slaves for 430 years. Whatever was left was to be burned the next morning.

They were to eat the Passover meal with their sandals on, their cloak tucked into their belt, and holding their staff (10:11). This was to show they were ready to leave and to follow God wherever he was taking them.

God gave Moses further instructions to the Israelites about the Passover being a yearly remembrance of this event forever. He told Moses to tell the people that they were to let their children, grandchildren, and all future generations know why they celebrate the Passover and what it means. When Moses had finished telling them all that God had said, they worshipped God and set about doing just what they were told to do.

The death angel

At midnight on the night of the first Passover meal, God sent the death angel to kill every firstborn in every Egyptian family. We read in 12:30 that there was not a house in Egypt without someone dead...including Pharaoh's house.

When Pharaoh realized his firstborn son had died, he called Moses and Aaron to him in the middle of the night. He told them to go and to take whoever and whatever they wanted...just GO!

Moses and Aaron spread the word to the Israelites that they were leaving.

They also told them (as they had been instructed by God to do) to ask the Egyptians for silver, gold, and items of clothing to take with them. The Egyptians were more than happy to give them whatever they wanted as long as they left.

The first steps forward

Sometime during the wee hours of the night or early in the morning following the plague of death on the firstborn, 600,000 Israelite men plus their wives and children, all their livestock, their unleavened bread dough, and several other people (12:38) left Egypt headed for Sinai.

NOTE: Moses did not leave, however, without taking the bones of Joseph. He did this because even though Joseph was highly respected in Egypt, he knew that someday God would want to take his people back where they belonged. So for this reason, he made his brothers promise that when that day came, his bones would be taken back to where he had come from, too. This request was obviously passed down through the generations and honored by Moses.

God led the people himself. He took the form of a distinct cloud-like pillar by day and a pillar of fire by night in the sky. The first place they camped was in Succoth and from there God led them to Etham and then on to Migdol (or near there) on the shores of the Red Sea. God purposefully took them on this longer route to avoid Philistine cities. He did so because he knew the Israelites were not yet capable of defending themselves. They had been slaves for centuries. They were physically and mentally unequipped for fighting back, which is what they most likely would have had to do.

Along the way God also gives Moses and Aaron instructions for how they are to commemorate this event and for dedicating every firstborn head of livestock and their own children to the LORD.

A parting of the ways by way of the water

In chapter 14 we learn that Pharaoh's grief is short-lived and that when he realizes that the Israelites (free labor) are really gone, he sends his army after them to bring them back. At this point the Israelites are camped at the shores of the Red Sea. When they realize that Pharaoh's army is nearly upon them, they become scared and angry. This is the first of what will be MANY times the Israelites lash out at Moses; blaming him for their troubles. This time they basically tell him they were better off being slaves than being pursued by Pharaoh's army. Moses responds by assuring them that God will protect them. In 14:14 Moses speaks words that we all need to hold close to our heads and hearts every single day of our lives...

The LORD will fight for you; you need only to be still.

God, who had been leading by way of the cloud, moved from in front of them to behind them—blocking the Egyptian army's view of the Israelites and making it too dark for them to see. The people spent the night like this, all while God sent an east wind to part the waters after Moses raised his staff, so that when morning came, every Israelite man, woman, and child, every head of livestock and whoever else had come with them crossed over to the other side on dry ground.

This took some time. With that many people and animals, it had to take several hours. So where was Pharaoh's army while this was going on? God made their horses agitated, the wheels fell off their chariots...in short they were a mess.

Once everyone was safely across, however, some of Pharaoh's army went in after them while others turned around and were heading back home because of their fear of the LORD. It was at that point that God told Moses to stretch out his staff again over the water to move it back into place. When this happened, all of Pharaoh's men, horses, and chariots that were in or near the water were drowned.

The Israelites were in awe of what God had done for them through Moses and they worshipped God and vowed to put their trust in him and in Moses.

BRIAN GUGAS

Traveling Mercies

Chapters 15-17 provide us with information about the early days of the Israelite's journey out of Egypt. Following the drowning of Pharaoh's army when God collapsed the walls of water down on them, putting the Red Sea 'back in place', Moses and Aaron's sister, Miriam, led the women in singing and dancing in praise to God for his protection. Following this time of praise and worship we read about several important events that provide us with valuable insight to God's nature and the nature of the people he calls his.

Moses leads the people on a 3 day hike through the desert of Shur. For 3 long days the people travel across the wilderness of Shur (the NIV uses the word 'desert' of Shur) without finding any water to drink. When they finally do find water on that third day of their travels, they cannot drink it because it is 'bitter'.

The fact that the water was bitter (most likely brackish or too salty) was not unusual. Much of the water around that area was like that. It was also no mistake or coincidence that this is the type of water they came to. God purposefully led them to Marah (bitter water) to once again prove his constant TLC toward them by instructing Moses to toss a piece of wood lying nearby into the water. When Moses did what God told him to do, the water became fresh and drinkable.

Afterwards, God told the people that if they would listen carefully, follow his leading, and obey his commands without question, he would keep them free of all diseases (15:26). There is, however, no mention made of the people's response to God's instruction, which is both sad and unfortunate. It should also serve as a reminder to you and me.

God purposefully put the people of Israel into a situation in which they could not help themselves in order to prove he will always be there to care for them and provide their needs. Now while he doesn't have us throwing sticks into water these days, he is still teaching us the same lessons today. He just uses different 'lesson plans'.

After the water is made clean, Moses leads them to Elim where they find 70 palm trees and sall the fresh water they wanted. After staying there for nearly 2 weeks (approx.), they continued traveling toward Sinai by way of the Desert of Sin. Here is where we find them grumbling about a lack of food. No worries, God says, and in chapter 16 we read about the quail God provide for them each evening and the manna God provided each and every morning for them to eat for 40 years.

In this chapter we also see another instance in which God gives specific instructions to be followed (a test of faith and obedience) and the Israelites' inability or unwillingness to do so.

NOTE: It is easy for us to read these verses and tsk-tsk the Israelites for their lack of faith. But are we any better? Sure, they had the concrete evidence of God's handiwork, but don't we?

Chapter 17 tells us about two important incidents:

The people are in need of water again, they are grumbling and complaining about their situation, and God patiently provides by having Moses hit a rock with his staff in order to make water gush out of the rock.

The Israelites have their first encounter with an enemy…the Amalekites.

The battle between Israel and the Amalekites is significant for several reasons:

This is the first time we 'meet' Joshua, who will become the leader of the Israelites after Moses' death.

We are introduced to Hur. While Hur is not mentioned very often, it is evident he is respected and has a considerable amount of authority within the Israelite community.

God performs another miracle (17:8-13) in the way he brings victory to the Israelites over the Amalekites.

Quite honestly, only a miracle would have allowed a group of untrained, unprepared, and ill-equipped people to win against a trained army.

God tells Moses to write down the details of this event to save for future generations.

NOTE: This is the second time God has instructed Moses to preserve something for history's sake—the first being the manna he was told to store away (16:33-36).

Chapter 18 re-introduces us to Moses' wife, sons, and father in-law. We are told that Moses' wife, Zipporah, along with their two sons, Gershom and Eliezer, and Jethro, who is Zipporah's father, meet up with Moses and the rest of the Israelites in the desert. This is the first mention of Zipporah and the boys since the night they left to go to Egypt—the night she circumcised Eliezer. So why were they back with Jethro and when did they go?

The answer to the question of 'why' is obvious. Moses needed someone to care for his family in his absence and who better than Jethro? Jethro was a wise, loving, and good man who feared God (even though he was a Midianite). As for the answer to when they returned to

Jethro's household, we don't really know. Most assume it was after the night of Eliezer's circumcision due to the fact that he would have needed time to heal; making traveling to Egypt nearly impossible. Others believe that was only part of it. Some believe that Zipporah was so angry over having to do that to her youngest son that she refused to go any farther with her husband. It doesn't really matter what we think happened, though, because we don't know so it must not matter. What' matters in chapter 18 is this:

Jethro, being a man who has held positions of authority, observes the tremendous 'work load' Moses is putting on himself by being the sole judge and jury for the Israelites, and offers up a suggestion for making things easier while not diminishing the outcome. He proposed that Moses not be the one and only person who would hear the people's complaints and problems and offer resolution. He proposed that Moses choose wise, Godly men to serve as judges in varying degrees, with Moses hearing only the most serious cases.

Moses agreed Jethro was spot-on and did just that.

Jethro left Zipporah and the boys with Moses and returned to Midian.

Moses and the others arrived at the foot of Mt. Sinai three months to the day after they left Egypt.

The journey from Egypt had been eventful, to say the least, but that was nothing compared to what was yet to come....

BRIAN GUGAS

The Commandments, the Law, and the Tabernacle

Chapters 19-24 focus on the Mosaic Law as God gave it to Moses. We know that the book of Leviticus is considerably more specific in spelling out everything God said—and we will get to that in the next book in this series. For now, however, we will focus on God's appearing to the people of Israel, his speaking to Moses, and some of the basic elements of the laws God gave Israel.

The events took place as follows:

God called out to Moses on Mt. Sinai and gave him a message to give to the people of Israel. The message was this: Now if you will obey me fully and keep my covenant, then out of all nations you will be my treasured possession. Although the whole earth is mine, you will be for me a kingdom of priests and a holy nation." (19:5-6).

NOTE: This is the first time in the Bible that the word 'kingdom' is used in reference to Israel. This is the beginning of what is called the theocratic kingdom;

meaning the kingdom in which God rules as the supreme authority.

Moses told the people what God had said and they ALL agreed they would do whatever God asked of them.

Moses goes back up the mountain to tell God what the people said.

God tells Moses he is going to allow the people to hear him (God) speak to Moses and to come into sight for all the people to see, BUT Moses was to put up strict boundaries around the base of the mountain because anyone who go too close or touch the base of the mountain would die and the people were required to purify themselves for 3 days before this could take place.

Verses 16-19 describe how God's presence looked and sounded to the Israelites.

God tests Moses to see if he and the Israelites understood his instructions regarding boundaries they were to stay within.

Chapter 20 opens with God giving Moses the Ten Commandments for the first time.

The people were so afraid and humbled by what they saw that they didn't want God to speak to them. Moses reassures them that God is on their side.

God gives Moses another message for the Israelites: to not make or worship any gods other than him.

NOTE: To not have or worship any gods but God is the first commandment and the only commandment he referenced in his message to the Israelites before getting into the nitty-gritty of the Law. What does this say to you? To me it says that God knows us too well. He knows how easily swayed we are by Satan's attempts to lure us away from the truth.

The Law

The first laws God speaks to Moses about concern the subject of sacrifices. On the subject of sacrifices God first addresses the issue of building an altar. He gives Moses two basic instructions for doing so if building one out of rocks (stones).

Don't 'dress' the stones. In other words, don't chip away at them to make them fit together better or cut designs in them. He wants plain, uncut stones...just the way he made them.

Don't elevate it to the point of having to climb stairs to get to it. God didn't want anyone to expose their nakedness (genitals) to anyone who might be standing below. Remember...this was pre-underwear days.

The fact that God mentions sacrifices first should be a reminder to us that God should always come first and that we should give the first of everything we have to him.

Next God talks to Moses about the relationships between masters and slaves. Chapter 21 begins with instructions regarding Hebrew slaves and Hebrew masters. This seems completely contradictory and out of character seeing as how they had just been freed from 400 years of oppressive conditions as slaves in Egypt. Apparently, though, the practice of indentured slavery was very common among the Israelite (Jewish) people. Slavery other than indentured slavery was also common with the Israelites. Most non-indentured slaves were the result of taking prisoners of war, but that was not always the case. And we must remember that at this point in time, they hadn't experienced warfare yet so they had no prisoners of war. Therefore, we need to understand that slavery did exist among the people of Israel—indentured and otherwise. If it didn't, God wouldn't have seen a need to address it and he wouldn't have made it the second-most priority on the list.

NOTE: Not only does the Bible address the issue, but the Talmud and the Torah also address the issue in the same manner the Bible does.

NOTE: Indentured slavery is working for someone without pay for a specified period of time in order to pay off a debt or pay for damages done to someone else's property. Think back to Jacob, Leah, and Rachel. Jacob worked for Laban for 14 years in order to 'earn' the right to marry his beloved Rachel.

Following the instructions on master/slave relationships God addresses personal injuries. He covers:

Kidnapping

Murder

Injury to a pregnant woman

Children attacking their parents

Throwing stones at one another (literally)

Being gored by a bull (which would have been a real problem in those days)

Injuries that disable someone

Injuries to another's livestock

Next God deals with property rights. These laws include laws about several situations including:

Breaking and entering

Theft

Trespassing

Destruction of another's property

Crimes against humanity are next on God's agenda. This includes:

Seducing and sleeping with a virgin

Sorcery and witchcraft

Having sex with animals

Idol worship

Racism or mistreating people who are different from you culturally/ethnically

Taking advantage of those who are less fortunate and in need

Lending/borrowing

Blaspheme

Tithing

Gossip

Keeping things that don't belong to you

Fairness and true justice

God's instructions to Moses regarding crimes against humanity cover a wide variety of situations, but there is one he mentions twice directly and indirectly another time. What is it? It is the crime of what we would call racism. God warns the people of Israel to not oppress an alien because they were once aliens in Egypt. He tells them to remember what it felt like for them to be mistreated and to never subject another person to that kind of treatment.

Now I know some may find this perplexing due to the fact that later on God instructed the Israelites to be so ruthless in annihilating everyone in order to take the Promised Land as their own. But here's the deal... With God it is all or nothing. God knew the Israelites would not be able to truly serve him with their whole hearts and minds in a culture of idol worship. Because he so desperately wanted the Israelites to be his people...his kingdom, he instructed them to purge all sin and temptation from their lives in order to be those people...that kingdom.

This is different than mistreating an alien, as God calls them, in the fact that just because someone is different from you doesn't make them bad. It makes them different. It also makes them someone we should reach out to in love as we are called to love. But when someone (or several someones) is trying to turn you away from God or destroy his Church, God expects us to fight for his Church. What I want you to understand from all of this is God's instructions and actions toward the

Canaanites, Philistines, and so forth weren't about the color of their skin or where they were born. It was about SIN. It was about their unwillingness to accept God and their determination to defile him however and whenever they could.

I know a lot of what God does throughout the Old Testament is difficult to comprehend, but that's where faith comes in; believing and knowing God's way is always perfect and purposeful and that when we allow him to, we will always be able to realize the goodness of his ways in our lives.

Now let's move on to the land and the Sabbath. God introduces his plan for the people's observance of the Sabbath and the treatment of their land by telling Moses that the people are to let their land rest every seventh year and to observe the Sabbath day as a day of rest just as he did. He ends this with yet another reminder to not worship or make idols and gods.

NOTE: As I read these reminders my heart breaks for God's heart. He reminded Moses of the dangers of idol worship over and over knowing his beloved people would not listen.

From here God gives Moses instructions regarding the three festivals of celebration to God. They are:

The Feast of Unleavened Bread—in the month of Nisan (Abib)

The Feast of the Harvest—when the first fruits of the crops sown each year

The Feast of Ingathering—the end of the year when crops are gathered

God also instructs Moses to tell the people that they are never to offer a blood sacrifice or anything containing yeast to him at these times.

From here God moves on to instructions AND promises about conquest of the land. This is the first time God combines instructions with promises. He does so because taking the Promised Land as their own isn't going to be easy. God knows that. He also knows that the Israelites are not capable of doing so without his divine intervention. In this section of scripture (23:20-33) God says the following:

He is providing an angel to lead the way and guard the way to the Promised Land.

He warns Moses that the people must obey the angel explicitly because his NAME is in him. The Hebrew word used for 'in him' means to be part of or entered into. In other words, this angel had the spirit of God in him.

He lists the people Israel will wipe out with God's divine intervention.

He warns them against worshipping the gods of the people they are going to go up against.

He instructs Moses to destroy the false gods.

He PROMISES the following in return for Israel's complete obedience and worship:

Blessing on their food and water

No sickness, infertility, or miscarriages

A full life-span; meaning they would not experience the ailments of aging, but would just pass away at the end of their life

He shares a snippet of his battle plan with Moses

And once again he warns Moses against making a covenant with any of the people they will be in confrontation with because if they do these people will cause Israel to sin against God.

Worship and the tabernacle

Chapter 24 begins with God telling Moses to get Aaron, Aaron's sons, Nadab and Abihu, and 70 of the elders of Israel to come up on the mountain with him to worship. BUT, he warns, they are to keep their distance when Moses approaches God and the rest of Israel is to stay put.

When Moses tells the people what God wants, they immediately respond that they will do exactly as God wants them to.

The following morning Moses built an altar, offered a sacrifice to God then proceeded to read the Book of the Covenant to the people. NOTE: the Book of the Covenant is what God had just dictated to Moses.

In 24:9-14 we see Moses, Aaron, Nadab, Abihu, and the 70 elders of Israel meeting God on the mountain. While they did not see all of God, we are told they saw his feet standing on a sapphire pavement. We read that God allowed them to do this without dying because they were so near his presence. God even allowed them to eat and drink (24:11).

Next God calls Moses to come up even higher on the mountain with him so that he (God) can give Moses the tablets containing the commandments and laws God has written for the people of Israel. At this point we are first introduced to

Joshua. He is described as Moses' aide. He and Joshua proceed up the mountain; leaving Aaron, Hur, and the elders to handle all the disputes that might break out among the people. For six days Moses and Joshua stayed on the mountain near a thick cloud, which was the glory of the LORD (24:15). But on the seventh day the LORD called Moses to come to him. Moses then entered the cloud and remained there with God for 40 days and 40 nights.

During this time God speaks to Moses regarding the tabernacle and the order of worship. But God does more than 'just' speak to Moses. God writes down explicit instructions on how he expects things to be done. Several verses in chapters 25-31 tell us that God wrote these laws and instructions with his own finger and that he showed Moses a pattern (drawing) for how he wanted the tabernacle constructed. WOW!

I am not going to go into great detail here because it would simply take too long. Instead I am going to give you the broad overview. I do, however, strongly encourage you to read these chapters for yourself in order to take in the magnitude of detail and preciseness God put into what he wanted Moses to do.

Materials for the tabernacle

God instructs Moses to collect an offering from all the people whose heart prompts him to give. These offerings are to consist of gold, silver, bronze, linen, acacia wood, olive oil, blue, purple, and scarlet yarn, certain kinds of animal hides, certain kinds of precious gems, and certain kinds of spices.

BRIAN GUGAS

The Ark of the Testimony (Ark of the Covenant)

The first thing God instructed Moses to build was the Ark of the Testimony or Covenant. This was the container used to house the Testimony of the Covenant Moses had recently read to the Israelites, Ten Commandments, a gold jar of manna, and one of Aaron's staffs. God did not immediately tell Moses what would go into the Ark (except the Covenant of the Testimony). He simply said it would be used to hold "…which I will tell you…."

Two interesting things to note about the Ark are 1) it was to be carried without being touched. In order to do this, it would be built with hooks that would hold gold-covered wooden poles that were never to be removed from it and 2) the Ark was 3 ¾ feet long, 2 ¼ feet wide and 2 ¼ feet tall.

The Atonement Cover

God then told Moses the craftsmen would make an atonement cover out of gold to fit on top of the Ark. The atonement cover is a golden chair the same size as the Ark of the Testimony that sat over the top of the Ark. God told Moses to put the Covenant of the Testimony into the Ark, put the cover on top of it, place it in the prescribed place in the tabernacle, and then sit there for God to meet with him to give him the Law in detail.

It is important to understand the significance of the atonement cover because of what it does and what it represents. The word 'atonement' means propitiate or to re-gain favor. It is later referred to in Leviticus as the 'mercy seat' when blood is sprinkled on the chair; indicating it has gone from a seat of judgement to a seat of mercy.

Table of the Presence

This is a table made to God's specifications to be used to pour out special offerings to God and to hold the Bread of the Presence (manna) at all times in remembrance of God's provision to the Israelites.

The golden lampstand

Next on God's list is a golden lampstand made exactly to his specifications to be used to constantly burn oil to light parts of the tabernacle at all times.

Linen curtains, curtains of goat hair, ram skin coverings, frames and bases

God is now ready to give Moses explicit instructions for how the curtains (walls) of the tabernacle are to be made, what they are to be made of, and how they are to be joined together. The linen curtains are to be used for the interior walls, the goat hair curtains are the exterior walls, and the ram skins and sea cow hides are used to cover the walls— making it waterproof.

The dimensions of the bases and frames that will hold the curtains are given next. God leaves no detail out and everything is sized to perfection.

The set-up of the tabernacle

God explains to Moses how he wants the curtains assembled in regards to separating the Holy Place from the MOST Holy Place. He then continues by including instructions for the altar, the courtyard of the tabernacle and the entrance into the courtyard.

As I stated earlier, God left nothing...absolutely nothing to chance or speculation when it came to building the tabernacle. But that's not the only way in which God leaves nothing to speculation. He has been just as clear when it comes to what he wants from you and me.

Worship and the Priesthood

Chapter 28 begins with God's instructions to designate Aaron and his sons, Nadab, Abihu, and Eleazar as priest. But Aaron is to be the High Priest and is to be given special and sacred garments that will set him apart as someone with honor and dignity.

The entire chapter is dedicated to describing what is to be made for Aaron and how it is to be made. Prior to getting into the details, however, God states that those who make these garments are "...skilled men to whom I have given wisdom in such matters...." (28:3).

The most interesting and notable things we read about Aaron's garments are:

Much of the ornamentation revolves around recognizing the 12 tribes of Israel and is to be reminders of who Aaron is serving/leading.

The placement of these accessories is on his head and his heart—signifying the importance of the job he has been given.

God specifically makes note that the main robe is made in such a way that Aaron can take it on and off without tearing it.

Aaron's position makes him directly responsible for every offense and act of neglect against what God deems as "holy things".

Lesser garments are to be made for Aaron's sons to wear in their duties.

Underwear is to be made and worn by Aaron and his sons at all times when in the Tabernacle or in the meeting area. If they fail to do so, they will die.

From there we move into chapter 29 which explains the process of consecrating (ordaining) Aaron and his sons and the food they are to eat. This process involves 7 days of sacrifices and other rituals.

Chapter 30 begins God's instructions for worship in the tabernacle. These instructions include:

The building, use, and placement of the altar, burning of incense, and a warning to never duplicate the incense used on the altar for personal use.

God tells Moses who may worship him. He says the redeemed, the cleansed, and the anointed may worship him and describes how someone achieves the status of being redeemed, cleansed, and anointed.

Instruction is given as to prayer and praise. Once again, God warns Moses that the combination of spices offered up in praise to God cannot be used for anything else. Those who do must be cut off from the rest of Israel.

God and Moses are now coming close to the end of their 40 day/night time together. God ends their conversation by doing two things:

He tells Moses he has chosen Bezalel, the grandson of Hur, to be spirit-filled (31:3) in such a way that he will have extreme and exceptional knowledge and giftedness in the kinds of crafts and artistic matters and that he is doing the same for Oholiab from the tribe of Dan so that Oholiab can be Bezalel's assistant. These two are to be the overseers for the intricate craftsmanship God wants used in constructing the Ark, the tabernacle and the priestly garments.

God reminds Moses of the importance of the Sabbath.

When God is done speaking to Moses on Mt. Sinai, he presents Moses with two tablets written in his own hand.

Oh, but wait! God knows something Moses doesn't know…yet….

BRIAN GUGAS

Meanwhile, Back at the Base of the Mountain...

The Israelites proved to be less than patient and basically liars after only a few days of being left on their own (without Moses' leadership). They complained and whined that he had been gone too long and that they really didn't know if he would come back.

Really? As if seeing the cloud and fire on the mountain and hearing God's voice wasn't enough???

Aaron responded by telling them to give him their gold and jewelry, which he took and made an idol in the shape of a calf. Aaron saw that the people were basically worshipping the calf, so he told the people that the next day they would sacrifice to God and celebrate him.

God could see what was going on and became very angry. His anger was justified, of course, but God being God used it as a way to test Moses.

God told Moses what was happening and that his anger was so great that he was going to destroy them all, forget the promise he'd made to Abraham, and start over by making Moses into a great nation (32:10).

Oh, it would have been so easy for Moses to say, "Gee, thanks. That's really cool. I'd be glad to do that for you."

After all, Moses had already had to deal with a fair amount of whining and complaining. To be rid of all that responsibility and to have his family all to himself and it just be them and God out there would have been quite tempting. But not to Moses. Moses immediately asks God to reconsider. He reminds God of the promise he'd made to Abraham and how killing the Israelites would only 'prove' to the Egyptians just how wrong Israel had been in believing in you.

Moses passed the test, God relented and sent Moses on his way back down the mountain to deal with the people.

Joshua, who had been waiting somewhere between God/Moses and the people joined back up with Moses and commented that it sounded like Israel was in trouble—that they were fighting. Moses told Joshua that wasn't the case— that they were having a party.

When Moses saw just how out of control things had gotten and the gold calf idol, he became so angry that he threw down the tablets God had given him; shattering them to pieces. And to make matters worse, Aaron told a big, fat lie when confronted about the situation. Aaron told Moses that when the people had given him their jewelry he threw it into the fire and the calf had just magically appeared!

Thoroughly disgusted, Moses called out to the people asking that anyone who was for the LORD should come to him. Only the tribe of Levi did so. Giving them God's instructions, Moses told the Levites to strap a sword to them and walk through the people. Whoever they killed, they killed. The Levites did so and God blessed them for their obedience.

The next day Moses went to God to intercede for them and ask God to have mercy on them. God did have mercy, but not without discipline. God sent a plague on the people (we don't know what or for how long). God also said that he would still send the angel ahead of the Israelites to lead the way as they drove out all the people from the Promised Land, BUT he said he would not go with them.

Moses cannot let this rest. He knows they need God's presence in order to be victorious and for him to have any chance to keep these people focused on God. So in order to discuss this matter with God, Moses goes into the tent of meeting (something he was in the habit of doing) to call on God for help and wisdom.

We read in 33:11 that Moses would speak with the LORD face to face as one does with a friend. But then later in 33:19-23, we read that God had to cover Moses' face when he passed by so Moses wouldn't see God's face and die.

So what gives? Did Moses talk to God face to face or not?

The Hebrew word used in in verse 11 is 'panim' which can be translated both literally and figuratively. It can mean both a physical face AND a presence. In verse 11the translation can best be described as a one-on-one conversation. It was even more personal than what they had had before. It was more of a friend to friend rather than God to created one conversation.

The conversation they had was basically Moses telling God that if he (God) didn't go with them, he (Moses) didn't want to go either. Moses told God there was no need in them even going if God wasn't with them.

God's reply to Moses can be summed up like this: "Okay, I'll go but I'm not going because of them. I'm going because I love you and I don't want to let you down."

Chapter 34 opens with God telling Moses to chisel out two more tablets so God can re-write what he'd written on the first set. In order for him to do so Moses had to go back up on Mt. Sinai.

In re-writing the tablets God again reminds Moses of the importance of staying away from idol worship, the Sabbath, and the festivals he had instructed Moses on earlier.

When Moses came down from Mt. Sinai this time, again carrying tablets God had written on, his (Moses') face was glowing radiantly from being in God's presence. Aaron and the rest of the people were afraid to come near Moses because of the phenomena. Moses finally convinced them to come close enough to hear what he had to say and so they did. When he was done talking, though, he covered his face with a veil to shield everyone from the radiance of his face—only removing the veil when he went to speak to God.

The remainder of the book of Exodus (chapters 35-40) give us the account of the construction of the Ark of the Testimony, the tabernacle, and the garments to be worn by Aaron and his sons. Once everything was done according to God's explicit instructions, God took up residence in the Tent of the

Meeting where Moses had met with God until the tabernacle was done. From that point on, however, as long as the cloud (by day) or the pillar of fire (by night) rested on the Tent of the Meeting the people stayed camped where they were. But when the cloud/pillar lifted, the Israelites knew God was ready for them to move on.

BRIAN GUGAS

Final Thoughts on the Book of Exodus

Exodus is a book of both endings and beginnings. It is the ending of a time of prosperity for Israel in Egypt and an ending of God allowing his people to mistreat the Israelites. It is the beginning of bondage for Israel and a beginning of their freedom, as well.

Exodus is filled with examples of God's holiness, creativity, miraculous and divine interventions, and the revealing of God's extreme attention to detail.

God also takes an up-close and personal interest and interactive approach not really seen since the creation of the garden and Adam and Eve. But most of all, the book of Exodus introduces us to the fact that God will accept nothing but our all.

MY OTHER BOOKS (*Available on Amazon*) as Paperback or on Kindle as well

1) Bible Study Guide for Beginners

2) The Bible Book of Genesis Study Guide

3) The Bible Book of Leviticus Study Guide

4) Marriage Prayers

5) Thirty Quick Bible Studies That Will Change Your Life

6) Bible Study for Women

7) Bible Study Lessons – Women of The Bible

8) How to Memorize the Bible Scriptures and Verses

9) How to Study the Bible for Beginners

About the Author

Reach to me at: *briangugas@gmail.com*

Website: http://briangugas.com

Note **: You can subscribe to my mailing list by visiting my website (left hand sidebar above the BIBLE image) and you will get to know as and when I publish new books on Amazon**

You can Connect with me on Facebook as well